Crossword Bible Studies
The Gospel of John

King James Version

Crossword Bible Studies - The Gospel of John: King James Version
Copyright © 2012 Christy Bower
www.ChristyBower.com
ISBN-13: 978-1479146888
ISBN-10: 1479146889

Cover image © iStockphoto.com / Peter Nadolski
The 1611 edition of the King James Version (KJV) is in the public domain.

All clues are taken directly from the 1611 edition of the King James Version (KJV).
Crossword Bible Studies - The Gospel of John (KJV) © 2012 Christy Bower
These puzzles are reproducible if you purchased the book.
www.CrosswordBibleStudies.com

Thank You

Thank you for purchasing this volume of *Crossword Bible Studies*. You just put a meal on my table. And your support enables me to continue to produce other resources to help people grow in their faith.

Reproducible Puzzles

If you purchased this book, the author grants you the right to reproduce the puzzles for your family, church, or school. Please do not remove or alter the copyright information, instructions, and web address at the bottom of each page. You may not distribute digital copies and you may not resell either printed or digital copies.

Studying the Bible Can Be Fun

You'll have so much fun working these crossword puzzles; you'll never know it's a Bible study. Each puzzle is based on one chapter of the Bible and the clues are taken directly from the 1611 edition of the King James Version (KJV). The verse reference is provided with each puzzle clue, so all you have to do is look up the answer in your Bible.

Don't have a KJV? Check out www.ChristyBower.com to view, print, or download the text for each chapter or an entire book of the Bible.

Note: The clues are taken from the 1611 edition of the King James Version because it is in the public domain and free of copyright restrictions. Newer versions of the KJV have been edited over the years and may reflect slightly different wording in places. Be aware of this if you are looking up clues in a newer edition.

John 1 (KJV)

Across

3. For the law was given by _____ (1:17)
6. saith unto him, _____ me (1:43)
8. In him was _____; and the life was the light of men (1:4)
9. John bare _____ of him (1:15)
11. Can there any good thing come out of _____ (1:46)
14. _____, (which is to say, being interpreted, Master,) (1:38)
17. And the light shineth in _____ (1:5)
19. Philip findeth _____ (1:45)
20. Now _____ was of Bethsaida (1:44)
21. He was in the world, and the _____ was made by him (1:10)
22. He first findeth his own brother _____ (1:41)
23. The same came for a witness, to bear witness of the _____ (1:7)
24. In the _____ was the Word (1:1)

Down

1. Behold the _____ of God, which taketh away the sin of the world (1:29)
2. But as many as _____ him, to them gave he power to become the sons of God (1:12)
4. There was a man sent from God, whose name was _____ (1:6)
5. And the Word was made _____, and dwelt among us (1:14)
7. I am the voice of one crying in the _____ (1:23)
9. therefore am I come baptizing with _____ (1:31)
10. And the two disciples heard him speak, and they _____ Jesus (1:37)
12. angles of God _____ and descending upon the Son of man (1:51)
13. I saw the Spirit _____ from heaven like a dove (1:32)
15. _____, Simon Peter's brother (1:40)
16. Behold an _____ indeed, in whom is no guile (1:47)
18. I _____ with water (1:26)

All clues are taken directly from the 1611 edition of the King James Version (KJV).
Crossword Bible Studies - The Gospel of John (KJV) © 2012 Christy Bower
These puzzles are reproducible if you purchased the book.
www.CrosswordBibleStudies.com

John 1 (KJV)

John 2 (KJV)

Across

3. the governor of the feast called the _____ (2:9)
6. they _____ the scripture, and the word which Jesus had said (2:22)
9. Now when he was in _____ at the passover (2:23)
12. After this he went down to _____ (2:12)
13. And the Jews' _____ was at hand (2:13)
17. But Jesus did not _____ himself unto them (2:24)
18. And needed not that any should _____ of man (2:25)
19. poured out the changers' money, and _____ the tables (2:15)
22. there was a _____ in Cana of Galilee (2:1)
23. _____ this temple (2:19)
24. make not my Father's house an house of _____ (2:16)

Down

1. Destroy this temple, and in _____ days I will raise it up (2:19)
2. Fill the waterpots with _____ (2:7)
4. the mother of Jesus saith unto him, They have no _____ (2:3)
5. And when they wanted wine, the mother of _____ saith unto him (2:3)
7. set forth good wine; and when men have well _____, then that which is worse (2:10)
8. And when he had made a _____ of small cords (2:15)
10. This beginning of _____ did Jesus in Cana of Galilee (2:11)
11. And his disciples _____ that it was written (2:17)
14. And found in the temple those that _____ oxen and sheep and doves (2:14)
15. Draw out now, and bear unto the governor of the _____ (2:8)
16. But he spake of the temple of his _____ (2:21)
20. And there were set there six _____ of stone (2:6)
21. he _____ them all out of the temple (2:15)
22. His _____ saith unto the servants, Whatsoever he saith unto you, do it (2:5)

John 2 (KJV)

John 3 (KJV)

Across

3. Except a man be born of water and of the _____, he cannot enter into the kingdom of God (3:5)
5. And John also was _____ (3:23)
8. a question between some of John's _____ and the Jews (3:25)
9. should not perish, but have _____ life (3:16)
12. shall not see life; but the _____ of God abideth on him (3:36)
14. He that hath the bride is the _____ (3:29)
18. men loved _____ rather than light (3:19)
19. He must increase, but I must _____ (3:30)
20. The Father loveth the Son, and hath _____ all things into his hand (3:35)
23. Except a man be born again, he cannot see the _____ of God (3:3)
24. That which is born of the flesh is _____ (3:6)

Down

1. A man can _____ nothing, except it be given him from heaven (3:27)
2. For John was not yet cast into _____ (3:24)
3. but that the world through him might be _____ (3:17)
4. _____ and his disciples (3:22)
6. And no man hath _____ up to heaven (3:13)
7. And as Moses lifted up the serpent in the _____ (3:14)
10. I am not the _____, but that I am sent before him (3:28)
11. How can a man be _____ when he is old (3:4)
13. For God sent not his Son into the world to _____ the world (3:17)
15. That whosoever believeth in him should not _____, but have eternal life (3:15)
16. no man receiveth his _____ (3:32)
17. Rabbi, we know that thou art a _____ come from God (3:2)
21. There was a man of the Pharisees, named _____ (3:1)
22. For every one that doeth evil hateth the _____ (3:20)

All clues are taken directly from the 1611 edition of the King James Version (KJV).

Crossword Bible Studies - The Gospel of John (KJV) © 2012 Christy Bower
These puzzles are reproducible if you purchased the book.

www.CrosswordBibleStudies.com

John 3 (KJV)

John 4 (KJV)

Across

2. Except ye see signs and _____, ye will not believe (4:48)
4. having seen all the things that he did at _____ at the feast (4:45)
6. worship the Father in spirit and in _____ (4:23)
7. Jesus therefore, being _____ with his journey (4:6)
10. Go, call thy _____, and come hither (4:16)
12. shall be in him a well of water springing up into _____ life (4:14)
13. And there was a certain _____, whose son was sick at Capernaum (4:46)
16. Yesterday at the seventh hour the _____ left him (4:52)
18. from whence then hast thou that _____ water (4:11)
19. his _____ met him, and told him, saying, Thy son liveth (4:51)
20. God is a _____ (4:24)
22. Whosoever drinketh of this water shall _____ again (4:13)
24. This is again the _____ miracle that Jesus did (4:54)
26. when ye shall neither in this _____, nor yet at Jerusalem, worship the Father (4:21)

Down

1. And many more believed _____ of his own word (4:41)
3. The woman then left her _____ (4:28)
5. And the man _____ the word that Jesus had spoken unto him (4:50)
8. heal his son: for he was at the point of _____ (4:47)
9. Sir, I perceive that thou art a _____ (4:19)
10. for we have _____ him ourselves (4:42)
11. for the Jews have no _____ with the Samaritans (4:9)
14. we know what we worship: for _____ is of the Jews (4:22)
15. look on the fields; for they are white already to _____ (4:35)
17. So the _____ knew that it was at the same hour (4:53)
21. Jerusalem is the place where men ought to _____ (4:20)
23. There cometh a woman of _____ to draw water (4:7)
25. Give me to _____ (4:10)

All clues are taken directly from the 1611 edition of the King James Version (KJV).

Crossword Bible Studies - The Gospel of John (KJV) © 2012 Christy Bower

These puzzles are reproducible if you purchased the book.

www.CrosswordBibleStudies.com

John 4 (KJV)

John 5 (KJV)

Across

3. said also that God was his Father, making himself _____ with God (5:18)
5. Search the _____; for in them ye think ye have eternal life (5:39)
9. the Father himself, which hath sent me, hath borne _____ of me (5:37)
14. I can of mine own self do _____ (5:30)
15. as the Father raiseth up the _____ (5:21)
18. For had ye believed _____, ye would have believed me (5:46)
21. believeth on him that sent me, that _____ life (5:24)
23. it is not _____ for thee to carry thy bed (5:10)
24. ye were willing for a season to _____ in his light (5:35)

Down

1. it was _____, which had made him whole (5:15)
2. all that are in the _____ shall hear his voice (5:28)
4. ye have not the _____ of God in you (5:42)
5. sought to slay him, because he had done these things on the _____ day (5:16)
6. ye have not his word _____ in you (5:38)
7. And a certain man was there, which had an _____ thirty and eight years (5:5)
8. hath given him _____ to execute judgment (5:27)
10. that ye might be _____ (5:34)
11. Take up thy _____, and walk (5:12)
12. ye will not come to me, that ye might have _____ (5:40)
13. they that have done good, unto the _____ of life (5:29)
16. Do not think that I will _____ you to the Father (5:45)
17. But if ye believe not his _____, how shall ye believe my words (5:47)
18. he will shew him greater works than these, that ye may _____ (5:20)
19. Jesus findeth him in the _____ (5:14)
20. Rise, take up thy bed, and _____ (5:8)
22. _____ up thy bed, and walk (5:11)

All clues are taken directly from the 1611 edition of the King James Version (KJV).

Crossword Bible Studies - The Gospel of John (KJV) © 2012 Christy Bower
These puzzles are reproducible if you purchased the book.

www.CrosswordBibleStudies.com

John 5 (KJV)

John 6 (KJV)

Across

1. his disciples _____ at it (6:61)
6. Two hundred pennyworth of bread is not _____ for them (6:7)
7. and when he had given thanks, he _____ to the disciples (6:11)
11. Have not I chosen you twelve, and one of you is a _____ (6:70)
12. I am that bread of _____ (6:48)
16. thou hast the words of _____ life (6:68)
17. I came down from _____, not to do mine own will (6:38)
20. not because ye saw the _____, but because ye did eat of the loaves, and were filled (6:26)
21. they see Jesus _____ on the sea (6:19)
23. I am the _____ bread which came down from heaven (6:51)
24. He spake of _____ Iscariot (6:71)
26. Gather up the _____ that remain (6:12)
27. So the men sat down, in number about five _____ (6:10)

Down

2. From that time many of his _____ went back (6:66)
3. take him by _____, to make him a king (6:15)
4. This is the work of God, that ye _____ on him whom he hath sent (6:29)
5. cometh down from heaven, and giveth life unto the _____ (6:33)
8. Then said Jesus unto the _____, Will ye also go away (6:67)
9. Jesus went up into a _____, and there he sat with his disciples (6:3)
10. every one which seeth the Son, and believeth on him, may have _____ life (6:40)
13. And when they had _____ him on the other side of the sea (6:25)
14. came to Capernaum, _____ for Jesus (6:24)
15. There is a lad here, which hath five _____ loaves, and two small fishes (6:9)
18. I am the _____ of life (6:35)
19. These things said he in the synagogue, as he taught in _____ (6:59)
22. Then they willingly _____ him into the ship (6:21)
25. It is I; be not _____ (6:20)

All clues are taken directly from the 1611 edition of the King James Version (KJV).
Crossword Bible Studies - The Gospel of John (KJV) © 2012 Christy Bower
These puzzles are reproducible if you purchased the book.
www.CrosswordBibleStudies.com

John 6 (KJV)

John 7 (KJV)

Across

1. When Christ cometh, will he do more _____ than these (7:31)
6. _____ saith unto them (7:50)
8. If any man _____, let him come unto me, and drink (7:37)
10. Are ye also _____ (7:47)
12. they sought to take him: but no man laid _____ on him (7:30)
13. Thou hast a _____: who goeth about to kill thee (7:20)
15. the chief priests sent _____ to take him (7:32)
18. he abode still in _____ (7:9)
21. no _____ is in him (7:18)
24. My _____ is not mine, but his that sent me (7:16)
25. Judge not according to the _____, but judge righteous judgment (7:24)

Down

2. Moses therefore gave unto you _____ (7:22)
3. this spake he of the _____, which they that believe on him should receive (7:39)
4. Why have ye not _____ him (7:45)
5. Then cried Jesus in the _____ as he taught (7:28)
7. then went he also up unto the feast, not openly, but as it were in _____ (7:10)
9. Go ye up unto this _____ (7:8)
11. So there was a _____ among the people because of him (7:43)
14. And every man went unto his own _____ (7:53)
16. out of his belly shall flow _____ of living water (7:38)
17. Jesus went up into the temple, and _____ (7:14)
19. Doth our law _____ any man, before it hear him, and know what he doeth (7:51)
20. Ye shall _____ me, and shall not find me (7:34)
22. Now the Jews' feast of _____ was at hand (7:2)
23. _____, and look: for out of Galilee ariseth no prophet (7:52)

All clues are taken directly from the 1611 edition of the King James Version (KJV).
Crossword Bible Studies - The Gospel of John (KJV) © 2012 Christy Bower
These puzzles are reproducible if you purchased the book.
www.CrosswordBibleStudies.com

John 7 (KJV)

John 8 (KJV)

Across

1. He that is without sin among you, let him first cast a _____ at her (8:7)
3. Whosoever committeth sin is the _____ of sin (8:34)
7. now ye seek to _____ me, a man that hath told you the truth (8:40)
8. Master, this _____ was taken in adultery (8:4)
9. Woman, where are thine _____ (8:10)
10. ye seek to kill me, because my _____ hath no place in you (8:37)
12. Jesus hid himself, and went out of the temple, going through the midst of them, and so _____ by (8:59)
13. the _____ of two men is true (8:17)
16. Jesus stooped down, and with his _____ wrote on the ground (8:6)
18. If the Son therefore shall make you _____, ye shall be free indeed (8:36)
19. If God were your Father, ye would _____ me (8:42)
21. again he stooped down, and wrote on the _____ (8:8)

Down

1. for if ye believe not that I am he, ye shall die in your _____ (8:24)
2. _____ is our father (8:39)
4. These words spake Jesus in the _____, as he taught in the temple (8:20)
5. Neither do I _____ thee: go and sin no more (8:11)
6. being convicted by their own _____, went out one by one (8:9)
7. If ye had _____ me, ye should have known my Father also (8:19)
9. Pharisees brought unto him a woman taken in _____ (8:3)
11. And because I tell you the truth, ye _____ me not (8:45)
14. Now Moses in the law commanded us, that such should be _____ (8:5)
15. I am the light of the _____ (8:12)
17. I seek not mine own _____ (8:50)
18. the _____ hath not left me alone (8:29)
20. And ye shall know the _____, and the truth shall make you free (8:32)

All clues are taken directly from the 1611 edition of the King James Version (KJV).

Crossword Bible Studies - The Gospel of John (KJV) © 2012 Christy Bower

These puzzles are reproducible if you purchased the book.

www.CrosswordBibleStudies.com

John 8 (KJV)

John 9 (KJV)

Across

3. We know that this is our son, and that he was _____ blind (9:20)
8. How can a man that is a sinner do such _____ (9:16)
10. made clay of the spittle, and he _____ the eyes of the blind man (9:6)
12. we know that God heareth not _____ (9:31)
13. he is of age; ask him: he shall speak for _____ (9:21)
15. they called the _____ of him that had received his sight (9:18)
19. Is not this he that sat and _____ (9:8)
22. Why herein is a marvellous thing, that ye _____ not from whence he is, and yet he hath opened mine eyes (9:30)
23. Since the world _____ was it not heard that any man opened the eyes of one that was born blind (9:32)
24. that the works of God should be made _____ in him (9:3)

Down

1. And they _____ him out (9:34)
2. A man that is called Jesus made _____, and anointed mine eyes (9:11)
4. it was the sabbath day when Jesus made the clay, and _____ his eyes (9:14)
5. he saw a man which was blind from his _____ (9:1)
6. He put clay upon mine eyes, and I _____, and do see (9:15)
7. Lord, I believe. And he _____ him (9:38)
9. I am the _____ of the world (9:5)
11. Who is he, Lord, that I might _____ on him (9:36)
14. For _____ I am come into this world, that they which see not might see (9:39)
16. Then they _____ him (9:28)
17. Go, wash in the pool of _____ (9:7)
18. the Jews had agreed already, that if any man did _____ that he was Christ, he should be put out of the synagogue (9:22)
19. whereas I was _____, now I see (9:25)
20. I have told you _____, and ye did not hear (9:27)
21. If this man were not of God, he could do _____ (9:33)

All clues are taken directly from the 1611 edition of the King James Version (KJV).
Crossword Bible Studies - The Gospel of John (KJV) © 2012 Christy Bower
These puzzles are reproducible if you purchased the book.
www.CrosswordBibleStudies.com

John 9 (KJV)

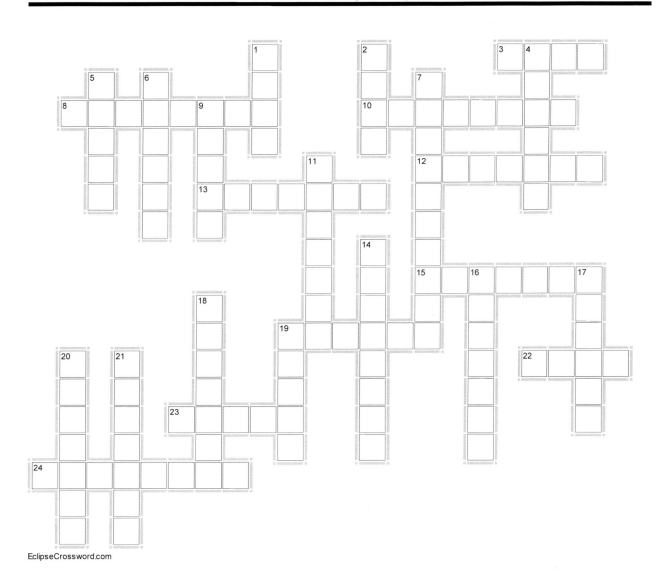

John 10 (KJV)

Across

2. If I do not the _____ of my Father, believe me not (10:37)
7. I give unto them _____ life (10:28)
11. This _____ have I received of my Father (10:18)
13. I am the _____ shepherd (10:11)
15. I and my _____ are one (10:30)
17. for they know not the voice of _____ (10:5)
19. Then the Jews took up _____ again to stone him (10:31)
21. But ye _____ not, because ye are not of my sheep (10:26)
22. for _____; and because that thou, being a man, makest thyself God (10:33)
23. they sought again to take him: but he _____ out of their hand (10:39)
25. no man is able to _____ them out of my Father's hand (10:29)

Down

1. the _____ catcheth them, and scattereth the sheep (10:12)
3. He that entereth not by the door into the _____ (10:1)
4. I lay down my _____ for the sheep (10:15)
5. My sheep hear my voice, and I know them, and they _____ me (10:27)
6. I am the good shepherd, and _____ my sheep (10:14)
8. the sheep follow him: for they know his _____ (10:4)
9. John did no _____: but all things that John spake of this man were true (10:41)
10. he that entereth in by the door is the _____ of the sheep (10:2)
12. I am the _____: by me if any man enter in, he shall be saved (10:9)
14. and the _____ cannot be broken (10:35)
16. I am come that they might have life, and that they might have it more _____ (10:10)
18. I am the door of the _____ (10:7)
20. And it was at Jerusalem the feast of the dedication, and it was _____ (10:22)
24. Jesus walked in the temple in Solomon's _____ (10:23)

All clues are taken directly from the 1611 edition of the King James Version (KJV).
Crossword Bible Studies - The Gospel of John (KJV) © 2012 Christy Bower
These puzzles are reproducible if you purchased the book.
www.CrosswordBibleStudies.com

John 10 (KJV)

John 11 (KJV)

Across

1. The Jews then which were with her in the house, and _____ her (11:31)
3. The _____ is come, and calleth for thee (11:28)
5. Now Jesus _____ Martha, and her sister, and Lazarus (11:5)
8. Lord, by this time he stinketh: for he hath been dead _____ days (11:39)
12. the _____ shall come and take away both our place and nation (11:48)
13. being high priest that year, he _____ that Jesus should die for that nation (11:51)
16. I am the _____ and the life (11:25)
19. Jesus _____ (11:35)
21. _____, come forth (11:43)
23. gather together in one the children of God that were _____ abroad (11:52)
24. But some of them went their ways to the _____, and told them what things Jesus had done (11:46)
25. it is expedient for us, that one man should die for the people, and that the whole _____ perish not (11:50)
26. I believe that thou art the _____, the Son of God (11:27)
27. Then said Jesus unto them plainly, Lazarus is _____ (11:14)

Down

2. Then said Thomas, which is called _____ (11:16)
4. he groaned in spirit, and was _____ (11:33)
6. and had seen the things which Jesus did, _____ on him (11:45)
7. Lord, if thou hadst been here, my _____ had not died (11:32)
9. Jesus therefore again _____ in himself cometh to the grave (11:38)
10. Martha and _____ (11:19)
11. Then said _____ unto Jesus, Lord, if thou hadst been here, my brother had not died (11:21)
14. This _____ is not unto death, but for the glory of God (11:4)
15. the Pharisees had given a _____, that, if any man knew where he were, he should shew it (11:57)
17. _____, the town of Mary and her sister Martha (11:1)
18. he that was dead came forth, bound hand and foot with _____ (11:44)
20. Our _____ Lazarus sleepeth (11:11)
22. the Jews of late sought to _____ thee; and goest thou thither again (11:8)
24. And the Jews' _____ was nigh at hand (11:55)

All clues are taken directly from the 1611 edition of the King James Version (KJV).

Crossword Bible Studies - The Gospel of John (KJV) © 2012 Christy Bower

These puzzles are reproducible if you purchased the book.

www.CrosswordBibleStudies.com

John 11 (KJV)

John 12 (KJV)

Across

3. Then took Mary a pound of ointment of spikenard, very costly, and _____ the feet of Jesus (12:3)
5. Yet a little while is the _____ with you (12:35)
7. they heard that Jesus was coming to _____ (12:12)
8. _____: Blessed is the King of Israel that cometh in the name of the Lord (12:13)
9. And I know that his _____ is life everlasting (12:50)
11. If any man serve me, let him _____ me (12:26)
13. now shall the _____ of this world be cast out (12:31)
16. whosoever believeth on me should not abide in _____ (12:46)
18. the chief priests consulted that they might put _____ also to death (12:10)
20. but because of the Pharisees they did not _____ him (12:42)
22. For they loved the _____ of men more than the praise of God (12:43)
23. Then Jesus six days before the passover came to _____, where Lazarus was (12:1)
24. Then came there a _____ from heaven (12:28)
26. there were certain _____ among them that came up to worship at the feast (12:20)
27. among the chief rulers also many _____ on him (12:42)

Down

1. Why was not this _____ sold (12:5)
2. for this cause came I unto this _____ (12:27)
4. and to whom hath the arm of the Lord been _____ (12:38)
6. The hour is come, that the Son of man should be _____ (12:23)
10. The people therefore, that stood by, and heard it, said that it _____ (12:29)
12. These things spake Jesus, and _____, and did hide himself from them (12:36)
14. that they might see Lazarus also, whom he had _____ from the dead (12:9)
15. when he called Lazarus out of his _____ (12:17)
17. He hath blinded their eyes, and _____ their heart (12:40)
19. though he had done so many _____ before them (12:37)
21. they did not confess him, lest they should be put out of the _____ (12:42)
25. There they made him a supper; and Martha _____ (12:2)

All clues are taken directly from the 1611 edition of the King James Version (KJV).
Crossword Bible Studies - The Gospel of John (KJV) © 2012 Christy Bower
These puzzles are reproducible if you purchased the book.
www.CrosswordBibleStudies.com

John 12 (KJV)

John 13 (KJV)

Across

2. laid aside his garments; and took a _____ (13:4)
6. Whither I go, thou canst not _____ me now (13:36)
7. there was _____ on Jesus' bosom one of his disciples (13:23)
10. The cock shall not crow, till thou hast _____ me thrice (13:38)
11. He then having received the sop went immediately out: and it was _____ (13:30)
13. that he should give _____ to the poor (13:29)
16. the _____ having now put into the heart of Judas Iscariot (13:2)
17. For he knew who should _____ him (13:11)
18. If I then, your Lord and Master, have _____ your feet (13:14)
19. he gave it to Judas _____ (13:26)
21. For I have given you an _____, that ye should do as I have done (13:15)
23. that the _____ may be fulfilled (13:18)
24. Thou shalt _____ wash my feet (13:8)

Down

1. A new _____ I give unto you (13:34)
3. he _____ them unto the end (13:1)
4. Little _____, yet a little while I am with you (13:33)
5. Lord, dost thou wash my _____ (13:6)
8. And after the sop _____ entered into him (13:27)
9. the _____ is not greater than his lord (13:16)
12. Then the disciples _____ one on another, doubting of whom he spake (13:22)
14. Lord, not my feet only, but also my _____ and my head (13:9)
15. Now before the feast of the _____ (13:1)
16. By this shall all men know that ye are my _____ (13:35)
20. Jesus knowing that the _____ had given all things into his hands (13:3)
22. After that he poureth _____ into a bason (13:5)

All clues are taken directly from the 1611 edition of the King James Version (KJV).
Crossword Bible Studies - The Gospel of John (KJV) © 2012 Christy Bower
These puzzles are reproducible if you purchased the book.
www.CrosswordBibleStudies.com

John 13 (KJV)

John 14 (KJV)

Across

3. I will not leave you _____: I will come to you (14:18)
5. the Father that dwelleth in me, he doeth the _____ (14:10)
8. that, when it is come to pass, ye might _____ (14:29)
9. If a man love me, he will _____ my words (14:23)
14. Even the _____ of truth (14:17)
16. In my Father's house are many _____ (14:2)
18. _____ saith unto him, Lord, we know not whither thou goest (14:5)
19. for the _____ of this world cometh (14:30)
22. he shall teach you all things, and bring all things to your _____ (14:26)
23. _____, let us go hence (14:31)
24. And if I go and prepare a _____ for you, I will come again (14:3)

Down

1. I am the way, the _____, and the life (14:6)
2. he shall give you another _____, that he may abide with you for ever (14:16)
4. he that loveth me shall be _____ of my Father (14:21)
6. If ye loved me, ye would _____ (14:28)
7. Let not your _____ be troubled (14:1)
10. _____ saith unto him, Lord, shew us the Father (14:8)
11. These things have I _____ unto you (14:25)
12. _____ works than these shall he do (14:12)
13. If ye love me, keep my _____ (14:15)
15. Have I been so long time with you, and yet hast thou not _____ me, Philip (14:9)
17. Yet a little while, and the _____ seeth me no more (14:19)
20. And whatsoever ye shall ask in my _____ (14:13)
21. _____ I leave with you (14:27)
23. If ye shall _____ any thing in my name, I will do it (14:14)

All clues are taken directly from the 1611 edition of the King James Version (KJV).
Crossword Bible Studies - The Gospel of John (KJV) © 2012 Christy Bower
These puzzles are reproducible if you purchased the book.
www.CrosswordBibleStudies.com

John 14 (KJV)

John 15 (KJV)

Across

2. for _____ me ye can do nothing (15:5)
3. If I had not done among them the _____ which none other man did (15:24)
5. These _____ I command you, that ye love one another (15:17)
6. Every _____ in me that beareth not fruit he taketh away (15:2)
7. so shall ye be my _____ (15:8)
11. that my joy might _____ in you (15:11)
15. But when the _____ is come, whom I will send unto you (15:26)
16. He that hateth me hateth my _____ also (15:23)
19. Ye have not chosen me, but I have _____ you (15:16)
20. As the branch cannot bear fruit of itself, except it _____ in the vine (15:4)
21. it _____ me before it hated you (15:18)
22. cast them into the fire, and they are _____ (15:6)
23. Now ye are clean through the word which I have _____ unto you (15:3)
24. Henceforth I call you not _____ (15:15)

Down

1. If they have _____ me, they will also persecute you (15:20)
2. And ye also shall bear _____, because ye have been with me from the beginning (15:27)
4. that the word might be fulfilled that is _____ in their law (15:25)
8. As the Father hath loved me, so have I _____ you (15:9)
9. They hated me without a _____ (15:25)
10. I am the true _____ (15:1)
12. If ye keep my _____, ye shall abide in my love (15:10)
13. I have chosen you out of the world, therefore the _____ hateth you (15:19)
14. Ye are my _____, if ye do whatsoever I command you (15:14)
17. That ye love one _____, as I have loved you (15:12)
18. _____ the word that I said unto you (15:20)

All clues are taken directly from the 1611 edition of the King James Version (KJV).
Crossword Bible Studies - The Gospel of John (KJV) © 2012 Christy Bower
These puzzles are reproducible if you purchased the book.
www.CrosswordBibleStudies.com

John 15 (KJV)

John 16 (KJV)

Across

1. In the world ye shall have _____ (16:33)
3. as soon as she is delivered of the child, she remembereth no more the _____ (16:21)
6. Of _____, because I go to my Father (16:10)
10. sorrow hath filled your _____ (16:6)
13. Then said some of his _____ among themselves (16:17)
16. ask, and ye shall _____ (16:24)
18. your heart shall _____, and your joy no man taketh from you (16:22)
19. Now _____ knew that they were desirous to ask him (16:19)
21. but be of good cheer; I have _____ the world (16:33)
22. because I go to the _____ (16:16)
23. ye shall be _____, but your sorrow shall be turned into joy (16:20)
24. Of _____, because the prince of this world is judged (16:11)
25. ye shall be _____, every man to his own, and shall leave me alone (16:32)

Down

2. Whatsoever ye shall ask the Father in my _____ (16:23)
4. for if I go not away, the _____ will not come unto you (16:7)
5. I leave the _____, and go to the Father (16:28)
7. He shall _____ me (16:14)
8. Of _____, because they believe not on me (16:9)
9. he will _____ the world of sin (16:8)
11. Do ye now _____ (16:31)
12. that ye should not be _____ (16:1)
14. when he, the _____ of truth, is come (16:13)
15. For the Father himself loveth you, because ye have _____ me (16:27)
17. ye may _____ that I told you of them (16:4)
20. They shall put you out of the _____ (16:2)

All clues are taken directly from the 1611 edition of the King James Version (KJV).

Crossword Bible Studies - The Gospel of John (KJV) © 2012 Christy Bower

These puzzles are reproducible if you purchased the book.

www.CrosswordBibleStudies.com

John 16 (KJV)

John 17 (KJV)

Across

2. and they have _____ thy word (17:6)
5. These words spake Jesus, and lifted up his eyes to _____ (17:1)
6. that the _____ might be fulfilled (17:12)
10. with the glory which I had with thee before the _____ was (17:5)
11. And the glory which thou gavest me I have _____ them (17:22)
12. the world hath not _____ thee (17:25)
13. keep through thine own _____ those whom thou hast given me (17:11)
14. and hast _____ them, as thou hast loved me (17:23)
15. I have glorified thee on the _____ (17:4)
18. I _____ not for the world, but for them (17:9)
19. thy _____ is truth (17:17)
21. and they have _____ that thou didst send me (17:8)
22. I have _____ thy name unto the men which thou gavest me (17:6)
24. that he should give _____ life to as many as thou hast given him (17:2)
25. I have _____ the work which thou gavest me to do (17:4)

Down

1. that they also might be _____ through the truth (17:19)
3. that they might know thee the only _____ God (17:3)
4. and the world hath _____ them, because they are not of the world (17:14)
7. for thou lovedst me before the _____ of the world (17:24)
8. I am _____ in them (17:10)
9. And I have _____ unto them thy name (17:26)
16. Neither pray I for these _____, but for them also which shall believe on me (17:20)
17. but that thou shouldest keep them from the _____ (17:15)
20. that they might have my joy _____ in themselves (17:13)
23. Sanctify them through thy _____ (17:17)

All clues are taken directly from the 1611 edition of the King James Version (KJV).
Crossword Bible Studies - The Gospel of John (KJV) © 2012 Christy Bower
These puzzles are reproducible if you purchased the book.
www.CrosswordBibleStudies.com

John 17 (KJV)

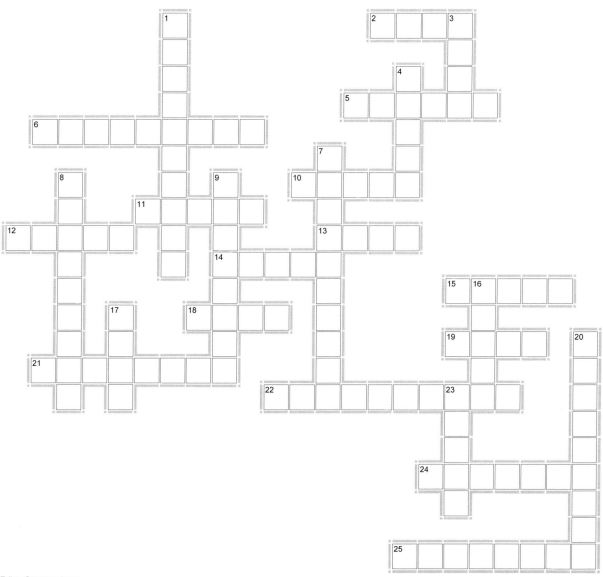

John 18 (KJV)

Across

5. Now Barabbas was a _____ (18:40)
7. He _____ it, and said, I am not (18:25)
8. _____ then denied again: and immediately the cock crew (18:27)
9. Did not I see thee in the _____ with him (18:26)
11. It is not lawful for us to put any man to _____ (18:31)
13. The high priest then asked Jesus of his disciples, and of his _____ (18:19)
16. Peter stood with them, and _____ himself (18:18)
18. Put up thy _____ into the sheath (18:11)
20. cometh thither with _____ and torches and weapons (18:3)
23. Art thou the _____ of the Jews (18:33)
24. that I should bear _____ unto the truth (18:37)
26. The servant's name was _____ (18:10)
27. And Simon Peter _____ Jesus (18:15)
28. Jesus of _____ (18:5)

Down

1. Not this man, but _____ (18:40)
2. What is _____ (18:38)
3. Then led they Jesus from Caiaphas unto the hall of _____ (18:28)
4. Now Annas had sent him bound unto _____ the high priest (18:24)
6. they went backward, and fell to the _____ (18:6)
10. And led him away to _____ first (18:13)
12. it was _____ that one man should die for the people (18:14)
14. for Jesus ofttimes _____ thither with his disciples (18:2)
15. I ever taught in the _____, and in the temple (18:20)
17. If he were not a malefactor, we would not have _____ him up unto thee (18:30)
19. Then went out that other _____, which was known unto the high priest (18:16)
21. What _____ bring ye against this man (18:29)
22. My _____ is not of this world (18:36)
25. he went forth with his disciples over the _____ Cedron (18:1)
27. I find in him no _____ at all (18:38)

All clues are taken directly from the 1611 edition of the King James Version (KJV).
Crossword Bible Studies - The Gospel of John (KJV) © 2012 Christy Bower
These puzzles are reproducible if you purchased the book.
www.CrosswordBibleStudies.com

John 18 (KJV)

John 19 (KJV)

Across

4. they cried out, saying, _____ him (19:6)
5. that the scripture might be fulfilled, saith, I _____ (19:28)
6. Mary _____ (19:25)
10. _____, which at the first came to Jesus by night (19:39)
12. knowest thou not that I have power to crucify thee, and have power to _____ thee (19:10)
14. And from thenceforth _____ sought to release him (19:12)
17. Then the _____, when they had crucified Jesus, took his garments (19:23)
18. Then Pilate therefore took Jesus, and _____ him (19:1)
19. But Jesus gave him no _____ (19:9)
20. But one of the soldiers with a _____ pierced his side (19:34)
23. a vessel full of _____ (19:29)
24. wearing the crown of thorns, and the _____ robe (19:5)
25. the place of a skull, which is called in the Hebrew _____ (19:17)

Down

1. When Jesus therefore saw his _____ (19:26)
2. Joseph of _____ (19:38)
3. When Pilate therefore heard that saying, he was the more _____ (19:8)
7. I find no _____ in him (19:4)
8. and in the garden a new _____, wherein was never man yet laid (19:41)
9. he said, It is _____: and he bowed his head, and gave up the ghost (19:30)
11. We have no king but _____ (19:15)
13. Then took they the body of Jesus, and wound it in _____ clothes (19:40)
15. And the soldiers platted a crown of _____, and put it on his head (19:2)
16. Thou couldest have no _____ at all against me, except it were given thee from above (19:11)
18. For these things were done, that the _____ should be fulfilled (19:36)
21. the judgment seat in a place that is called the _____, but in the Hebrew, Gabbatha (19:13)
22. that the bodies should not remain upon the cross on the _____ day (19:31)

All clues are taken directly from the 1611 edition of the King James Version (KJV).
Crossword Bible Studies - The Gospel of John (KJV) © 2012 Christy Bower
These puzzles are reproducible if you purchased the book.
www.CrosswordBibleStudies.com

John 19 (KJV)

John 20 (KJV)

Across

4. as my _____ hath sent me, even so send I you (20:21)
5. And seeth two _____ in white sitting (20:12)
10. And he _____ down, and looking in (20:5)
11. And after _____ days again his disciples were within (20:26)
12. seeth the _____ taken away from the sepulchre (20:1)
14. Except I shall see in his _____ the print of the nails (20:25)
17. _____; which is to say, Master (20:16)
21. supposing him to be the _____ (20:15)
22. and be not _____, but believing (20:27)
23. the doors were shut where the disciples were _____ for fear of the Jews (20:19)
24. Touch me not; for I am not yet _____ to my Father (20:17)

Down

1. Mary _____ (20:18)
2. But _____, one of the twelve, called Didymus (20:24)
3. Then the disciples went away again unto their own _____ (20:10)
6. For as yet they knew not the _____, that he must rise again from the dead (20:9)
7. Reach hither thy _____, and behold my hands (20:27)
8. but these are _____ that ye might believe that Jesus is the Christ (20:31)
9. then came Jesus, the _____ being shut, and stood in the midst (20:26)
10. she turned herself back, and saw Jesus _____ (20:14)
13. the other disciple did _____ Peter, and came first to the sepulchre (20:4)
15. he shewed unto them his hands and his _____ (20:20)
16. the other disciple, whom Jesus _____ (20:2)
18. he _____ on them, and saith unto them, Receive ye the Holy Ghost (20:22)
19. _____ be unto you (20:19)
20. Thomas, because thou hast seen me, thou hast _____, blessed are they that have not seen, and yet have believed (20:29)

All clues are taken directly from the 1611 edition of the King James Version (KJV).

Crossword Bible Studies - The Gospel of John (KJV) © 2012 Christy Bower
These puzzles are reproducible if you purchased the book.

www.CrosswordBibleStudies.com

John 20 (KJV)

John 21 (KJV)

Across

1. we know that his _____ is true (21:24)
4. Simon Peter saith unto them, I go a _____ (21:3)
6. and that night they caught _____ (21:3)
8. Feed my _____ (21:15)
11. the disciple whom Jesus _____ (21:20)
13. they saw a fire of _____ there, and fish laid thereon, and bread (21:9)
14. _____ my sheep (21:16)
15. taketh _____, and giveth them, and fish likewise (21:13)
17. This is now the _____ time that Jesus shewed himself to his disciples (21:14)
19. when the _____ was now come, Jesus stood on the shore (21:4)
20. _____ and dine (21:12)
21. Feed my _____ (21:17)
22. even the world itself could not contain the _____ that should be written (21:25)
23. So when they had _____, Jesus saith to Simon Peter (21:15)

Down

2. Simon, son of Jonas, lovest thou me more than _____ (21:15)
3. there are also many other things which _____ did (21:25)
4. Bring of the _____ which ye have now caught (21:10)
5. Yea, Lord; thou knowest that I _____ thee (21:16)
7. Peter was _____ because he said unto him the third time (21:17)
9. they were not able to draw it for the _____ of fishes (21:6)
10. he girt his fisher's coat unto him, (for he was _____) (21:7)
11. drew the net to _____ full of great fishes (21:11)
12. _____ the net with fishes (21:8)
16. Jesus shewed himself again to the _____ at the sea of Tiberias (21:1)
18. _____ thou me (21:22)

All clues are taken directly from the 1611 edition of the King James Version (KJV).

Crossword Bible Studies - The Gospel of John (KJV) © 2012 Christy Bower

These puzzles are reproducible if you purchased the book.

www.CrosswordBibleStudies.com

John 21 (KJV)

Solutions

John 1 (KJV)

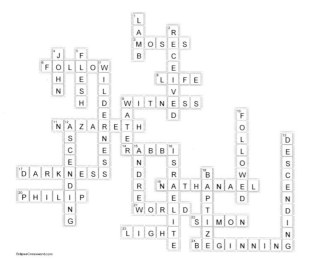

John 3 (KJV)

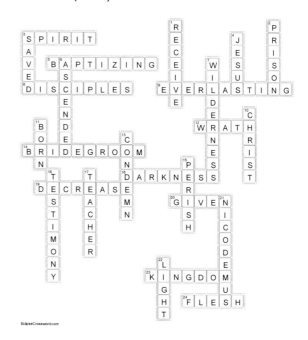

John 2 (KJV)

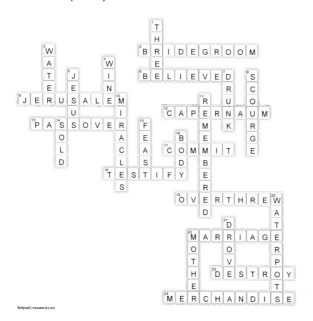

John 4 (KJV)

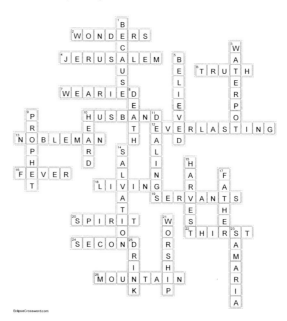

All clues are taken directly from the 1611 edition of the King James Version (KJV).
Crossword Bible Studies - The Gospel of John (KJV) © 2012 Christy Bower
These puzzles are reproducible if you purchased the book.
www.CrosswordBibleStudies.com

John 5 (KJV)

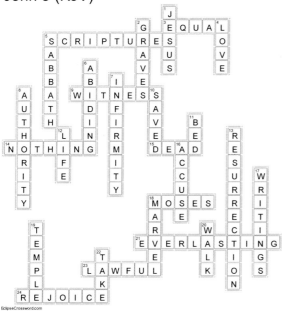

John 7 (KJV)

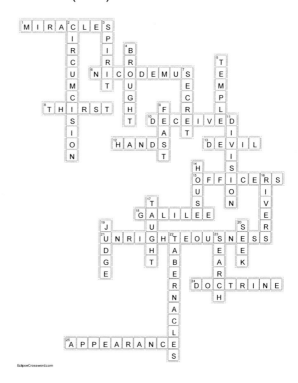

John 6 (KJV)

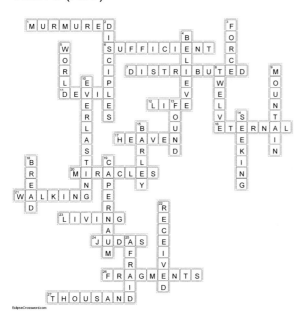

John 8 (KJV)

All clues are taken directly from the 1611 edition of the King James Version (KJV).
Crossword Bible Studies - The Gospel of John (KJV) © 2012 Christy Bower
These puzzles are reproducible if you purchased the book.
www.CrosswordBibleStudies.com

John 9 (KJV)

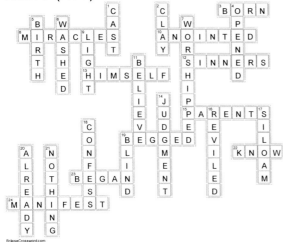

John 11 (KJV)

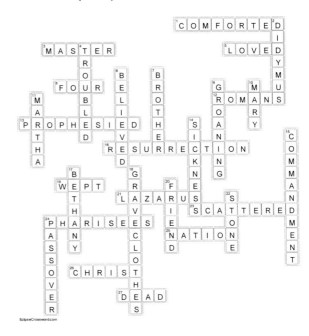

John 10 (KJV)

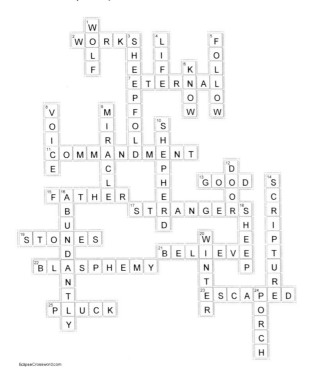

John 12 (KJV)

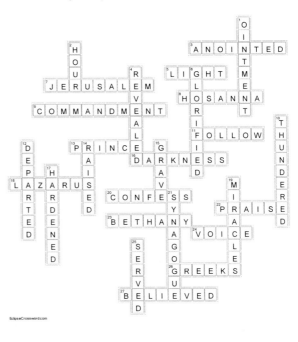

All clues are taken directly from the 1611 edition of the King James Version (KJV).
Crossword Bible Studies - The Gospel of John (KJV) © 2012 Christy Bower
These puzzles are reproducible if you purchased the book.
www.CrosswordBibleStudies.com

John 13 (KJV)

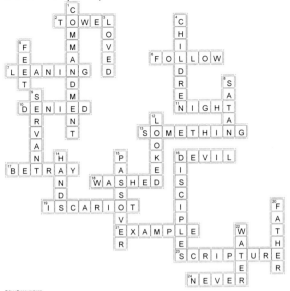

John 15 (KJV)

John 14 (KJV)

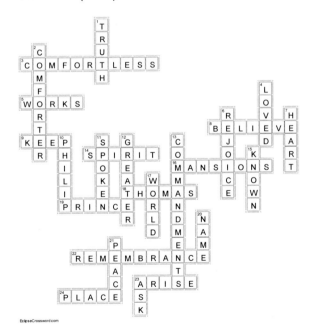

John 16 (KJV)

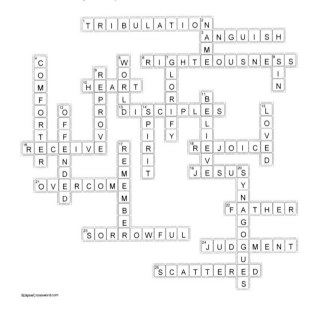

All clues are taken directly from the 1611 edition of the King James Version (KJV).
Crossword Bible Studies - The Gospel of John (KJV) © 2012 Christy Bower
These puzzles are reproducible if you purchased the book.
www.CrosswordBibleStudies.com

John 17 (KJV)

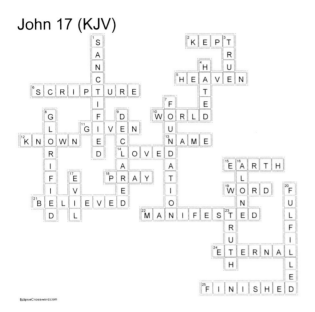

John 19 (KJV)

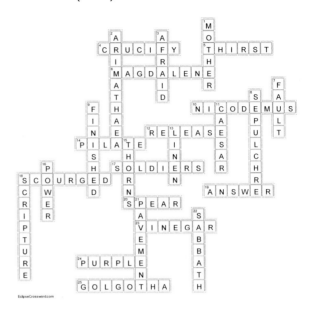

John 18 (KJV)

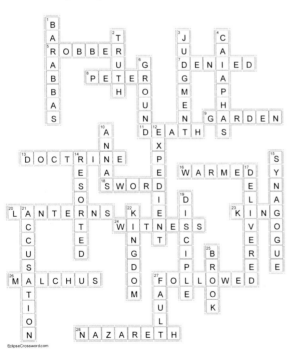

John 20 (KJV)

All clues are taken directly from the 1611 edition of the King James Version (KJV).
Crossword Bible Studies - The Gospel of John (KJV) © 2012 Christy Bower
These puzzles are reproducible if you purchased the book.
www.CrosswordBibleStudies.com

John 21 (KJV)

Made in United States
North Haven, CT
25 July 2023